W9-AHU-314

WISE WORDS FROM A WISE GUY

Vern McLellan

HARVEST HOUSE PUBLISHERS
Eugene, Oregon 97402

To my fun son, Kent,
who has a bent for wit and wisdom.

WISE WORDS FROM A WISE GUY
Copyright © 1989 by Vern McLellan
Published by Harvest House Publishers
Eugene, Oregon 97402

Library of Congress Cataloging-in-Publication Data

McLellan, Vernon K.
    Wise words from a wise guy / Vern McLellan.
    ISBN 0-89081-775-8
    1. American wit and humor.   2. Proverbs.   I. Title.
PN6162.M3485   1989
818' .5402—dc20   89-7630
                                                           CIP

Introduction

Francis Bacon once said, "The genius, wit, and spirit of a nation are discovered in its proverbs!" W.G. Benham commented that proverbs were "the wisdom of the streets." Cervantes once stated that a proverb was "a short sentence based on long experience."

On the pages of *Wise Words from a Wise Guy,* you'll read a wide variety of adages from sages of the ages—wisdom that has survived the centuries. I love proverbs—pithy, precise, often profound, thought-provoking sayings that effectively express some common-place truth or oft-repeated sayings.

Proverbial one-liners provide hooks on which you can happily hang truth. Many are humorous, which "helps the medicine go down more easily." I've watched audiences of all sizes and types burst into laughter as one of these proverbs lands. I hope you'll have the same experience repeatedly.

Other proverbs are confrontational, controversial, or conversational. Some will spark debate or hit like a ton of bricks. Others will sneak up on your funny side. Many are downright practical, pointed, and ponderable. Others challenge, cheer, and chart a change of lifestyle.

The Bible's Old Testament Book of Proverbs, a composite work completed about 250 B.C., brings balance to *Wise Words from a Wise Guy.* Noted inspirational speakers such as Dr. Billy Graham read a chapter a day from the timely, timeless Book of Proverbs and urges others to do the same.

Illustrator Sandy Silverthorne uses his artistic skills to blend the two proverbial types together.

I hope these wise, witty words—most of them anonymous—will add sparkle to your daily life and relationships.

—Vern McLellan

The golden rule:
He who has the gold
makes the rules . . .

Proverbs 22:7

Just as the rich rule the poor, so the borrower is servant to the lender.

He who travels the high road of humility is not troubled by heavy traffic . . .

Proverbs 16:18,19

Pride goes before destruction and haughtiness before a fall. Better poor and humble than proud and rich.

He who wins may have been counted out several times, but he didn't hear the referee . . .

Psalm 56:13

For you have saved me from death and my feet from slipping, so that I can walk before the Lord in the land of the living.

He *who thinks he knows*
it all is especially annoying
to those of us who do . . .

Proverbs 8:12,13

Wisdom and good judgment live together, for
wisdom knows where to discover knowledge and
understanding. If anyone respects and fears God,
he will hate evil. For wisdom hates pride, arrogance, corruption and deceit of every kind.

8

He who tries to whittle you down is only trying to reduce you to his size . . .

Proverbs 21:4,24

Pride, lust, and evil actions are all sin. Mockers are proud, haughty and arrogant.

He who engages in puppy love will live a dog's life . . .

Proverbs 25:28

A man without self-control is as defenseless as a city with broken-down walls.

He who boasts about his family tree should first do a good pruning job . . .

Proverbs 17:19

Boasting is looking for trouble.

He **who doesn't know whether he is coming or going is usually in the biggest hurry to get there . . .**

Proverbs 21:5

The plans of the diligent lead surely to advantage, but everyone who is hasty comes surely to poverty (NASB).

He who takes you to lunch even though he doesn't have an expense account is a real friend...

Proverbs 17:17

A true friend is always loyal, and a brother is born to help in time of need.

He who speaks without thinking is shooting without aiming...

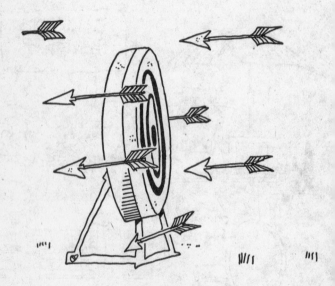

Proverbs 10:19,20

Don't talk so much. You keep putting your foot in your mouth. Be sensible and turn off the flow!

He who is patient in a moment of anger will escape a hundred days of regret...

Proverbs 19:11

A wise man restrains his anger and overlooks insults. This is to his credit.

He who wants a long friendship should develop a short memory...

Proverbs 18:19

It is harder to win back the friendship of an offended brother than to capture a fortified city. His anger shuts you out like iron bars.

He who invented the boomerang must also have invented the credit card...

Proverbs 15:16

Better a little with reverence for God, than great treasure and trouble with it.

He who doesn't know where he is going will discover that any road will take him there . . .

Proverbs 17:24

Wisdom is the main pursuit of sensible men, but a fool's goals are at the ends of the earth!

He who perishes by placing himself in needless danger is the devil's martyr...

Proverbs 14:6

A mocker never finds the wisdom he claims he is looking for, yet it comes easily to the man with common sense.

He who is already in the hole should stop digging . . .

Proverbs 14:16

A wise man is cautious and avoids danger; a fool plunges ahead with great confidence.

He who boos the loudest is probably sitting in one of the free seats . . .

Proverbs 17:27

He who restrains his words has knowledge, and he who has a cool spirit is a man of understanding (NASB).

He who has all his ducks in a row will not quack up...

Proverbs 16:9; Psalm 37:23

We should make plans—counting on God to direct us. The steps of good men are directed by the Lord. He delights in each step they take.

He who chooses a job he loves will never have to work a day of his life...

Proverbs 3:13-15

The man who knows right from wrong and has good judgment and common sense is happier than the man who is immensely rich! For such wisdom is far more valuable than precious jewels. Nothing else compares with it.

He who thinks at first glance that nothing can be done lacks courage and creativity . . .

Proverbs 18:14

A man's courage can sustain his broken body, but when courage dies, what hope is left?

He who tries to do today what he did 30 years ago can still do it—for 20 seconds!

Proverbs 20:29

The glory of young men is their strength; of old men, their experience.

He who loses his temper should not look for it . . .

Proverbs 14:29

A wise man controls his temper. He knows that anger causes mistakes.

He who thinks he's in the groove is often in a rut...

Proverbs 16:17,25

The path of the godly leads away from evil; he who follows that path is safe. Before every man there lies a wide and pleasant road he thinks is right, but it ends in death.

He who deals with a fox should consider his tricks . . .

Song of Solomon 2:15

"The little foxes are ruining the vineyards. Catch them, for the grapes are all in blossom."

He who drinks from the stream should remember the spring...

Psalm 92:1

It is good to say, "Thank you" to the Lord, to sing praises to the God who is above all gods.

He *who wants to leave footprints in the sands of time must wear work shoes...*

Proverbs 22:29

Do you know a hard-working man? He shall be successful and stand before kings!

He who has a dog to worship him should also have a cat to ignore him ...

Proverbs 15:33

Humility and reverence for the Lord will make you both wise and honored.

He *who sets aside two hours to do his income-tax return is an optimist...*

Proverbs 15:22

Plans go wrong with too few counselors; many counselors bring success.

He who has nothing to do has a real disadvantage: he can't stop and rest . . .

Proverbs 28:19

Hard work brings prosperity; playing around brings poverty.

He who puts his tongue into motion should be sure his brain is in gear...

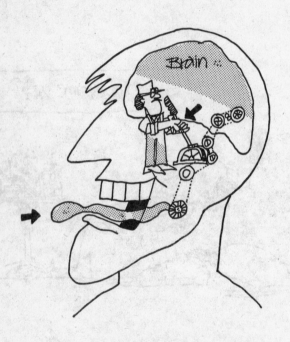

Proverbs 11:12

Proud men end in shame, but the meek become wise.

He who doesn't stand for something will fall for anything...

Proverbs 4:7

Determination to be wise is the first step toward becoming wise! And with your wisdom, develop common sense and good judgment.

One who burns the "scandle" at both ends is a busybody...

Proverbs 16:27

Idle hands are the devil's workshop; idle lips are his mouthpiece.

He who starts by saying, "Maybe I'm wrong," is often right...

Proverbs 28:13

A man who refuses to admit his mistakes can never be successful. But if he confesses and forsakes them, he gets another chance.

He *who feels dog-tired on Sunday morning needs to put God first on Saturday night...*

Proverbs 3:6

In everything you do, put God first, and he will direct you and crown your efforts with success.

He who plans to drink and drive should remember to kiss his mother good-bye . . .

Proverbs 21:16

The man who strays away from common sense will end up dead!

He who is kicked in the seat is out in front...

Ecclesiastes 12:11

The wise man's words are like goads that spur to action. They nail down important truths. Students are wise who master what their teachers tell them.

He who hesitates is last . . .

Ecclesiastes 11:4

If you wait for perfect conditions, you will never get anything done.

He who has a sharp tongue invites a split lip...

all I said was...

Proverbs 12:18

Some people like to make cutting remarks, but the words of the wise soothe and heal.

He who wants to get to the top must get off his bottom . . .

Proverbs 24:33,34

"A little extra sleep, a little more slumber, a little folding of the hands to rest" means that poverty will break in upon you suddenly like a robber, and violently like a bandit.

He who makes the least of the worst and the most of the best will reach the crest...

Job 17:9

The righteous shall move onward and forward; those with pure hearts shall become stronger and stronger.

He who gets ahead is the one who does more than is necessary—and keeps on doing it...

Proverbs 10:4

Poor is he who works with a negligent hand, but the hand of the diligent makes rich (NASB).

He who finds no fault in himself needs a second opinion...

Psalm 19:12

But how can I ever know what sins are lurking in my heart? Cleanse me from these hidden faults.

He who growls all day at you may be living with a bear...

Proverbs 15:4

Gentle words cause life and health; griping brings discouragement.

He who has no courage must have legs...

Proverbs 28:1

The wicked flee when no one is chasing them! But the godly are bold as lions!

He who never climbed never fell . . .

Psalm 145:14

The Lord lifts the fallen and those bent beneath their loads.

Those who complain about taxes can be divided into two classes: men and women . . .

Ecclesiastes 6:6

Though a man lives a thousand years twice over, but doesn't find contentment—well, what's the use?

He who will not sail until he has favorable winds will lose many a voyage . . .

Proverbs 19:3

A man may ruin his chances by his own foolishness and then blame it on the Lord!

He who marries for wealth sells his liberty . . .

Ecclesiastes 5:10

He who loves money shall never have enough. The foolishness of thinking that wealth brings happiness!

He who is lazy sticks his nose outside so the wind can blow it . . .

Proverbs 26:13,15

The lazy man . . . is too tired even to lift his food from his dish to his mouth!

He who cannot obey, cannot command...
—Benjamin Franklin

Proverbs 16:20

God blesses those who obey him; happy the man who puts his trust in the Lord.

He who blows his stack adds to the world's pollution...

Proverbs 15:18

A quick-tempered man starts fights; a cool-tempered man tries to stop them.

ℋe laughs best who laughs last . . .

Proverbs 15:13

A happy face means a glad heart; a sad face means a breaking heart.

He who has a right to boast doesn't have to . . .

Proverbs 14:24

Wise men are praised for their wisdom; fools are despised for their folly

He who is born of God should resemble his Father...

Daniel 2:21-23

He gives wise men their wisdom, and scholars their intelligence. He reveals profound mysteries beyond man's understanding. . . . I thank and praise you, O God of my fathers, for you have given me wisdom and glowing health.

He who prides himself on being hard-boiled is often only half-baked...

Proverbs 29:23

Pride ends in a fall, while humility brings honor.

He *who tells you to never let little things bother you has never tried sleeping in a room with a mosquito . . .*

Psalm 34:6

This poor man cried to the Lord—and the Lord heard him and saved him out of his troubles.

__He__ who learns and learns but acts not on what he knows, is like the one who plows and plows but never, never sows . . .

Proverbs 9:9

Teach a wise man, and he will be the wiser; teach a good man and he will learn more.

He who knows all the answers most likely misunderstood the questions . . .

Proverbs 2:3-5

Yes, if you want better insight and discernment, and are searching for them as you would for lost money or hidden treasure, then wisdom will be given you, and knowledge of God himself; you will soon learn the importance of reverence for the Lord and of trusting him.

He who continually looks down his nose at others usually has the wrong slant...

Proverbs 21:4,24

Haughty eyes and a proud heart, the lamp of the wicked, is sin. "Proud," "Haughty," "Scoffer," are his names, who acts with insolent pride (NASB).

He who wakes up and finds himself famous hasn't been asleep . . .

Proverbs 20:13

If you love sleep, you will end in poverty. Stay awake, work hard, and there will be plenty to eat!

He who plants his feet firmly in the dirt ends up with soiled socks...

Proverbs 13:20

Be with wise men and become wise. Be with evil men and become evil.

He who overeats knifes and forks himself to death...

Proverbs 23:19-21

... Be wise and stay in God's paths; don't carouse with drunkards and gluttons, for they are on their way to poverty.

He who arrives late for dinner must be content with leftovers . . .

Proverbs 19:15

A lazy man sleeps soundly—and goes hungry!

He **who talks too fast often says something he hasn't thought about yet . . .**

Proverbs 10:20

When a good man speaks, he is worth listening to, but the words of fools are a dime a dozen.

He who cannot wait for the apples to ripen will have a perpetual stomachache . . .

Proverbs 29:20

There is more hope for a fool than for a man with a quick temper.

He who has knocking knees should kneel on them...

Proverbs 3:25,26

You need not be afraid of disaster or the plots of wicked men, for the Lord is with you; he protects you.

He who cannot direct the winds can adjust his sails...

King's Ship

Romans 5:3

We can rejoice, too, when we run into problems
and trials for we know that they are good for us—
they help us learn to be patient.

He who does not come in out of the blinding snowstorm is flaky...

Proverbs 2:1,2

Every young man who listens to me and obeys my instructions will be given wisdom and good sense.

He who is flexible shall not be bent out of shape . . .

Be careful, he's a little bent out of shape this morning.

president

Proverbs 18:15

The intelligent man is always open to new ideas.
In fact, he looks for them.

He who meets temptation should turn to the right . . .

Proverbs 4:14-16

Don't do as the wicked do. Avoid their haunts—turn away, go somewhere else, for evil men don't sleep until they've done their evil deed for the day.

He whose troubles are all behind him is a school-bus driver...

Proverbs 15:3

The Lord is watching everywhere and keeps his eye on both the evil and the good.

He who is green with envy is ripe for trouble . . .

Proverbs 23:17

Don't envy evil men but continue to reverence the Lord all the time, for surely you have a wonderful future ahead of you.

He whose heart gives, gathers . . .

Proverbs 11:24,25

It is possible to give away and become richer! It is also possible to hold on too tightly and lose everything. Yes, the liberal man shall be rich! By watering others, he waters himself.

He who lies down on the job is up to his ears in work . . .

Proverbs 10:5

A wise youth makes hay while the sun shines, but what a shame to see a lad who sleeps away his hour of opportunity.

He who does a few good turns each day probably won't get dizzy...

Proverbs 21:21

The man who tries to be good, loving and kind finds life, righteousness and honor.

He *who thinks the boss is stupid would be out of a job if he were smarter...*

Proverbs 14:35

A king rejoices in servants who know what they are doing; he is angry with those who cause trouble.

He who finds life empty should try putting something into it . . .

Ecclesiastes 9:10

Whatever you do, do well, for in death, where you are going, there is no working or planning, or knowing, or understanding.

He who isn't afraid to go out on a limb will pick the fruit...

Proverbs 11:30

Godly men are growing a tree that bears life-giving fruit, and all who win souls are wise.

He *who says it can't be done shouldn't interrupt the man doing it...*

Proverbs 24:3,4

Any enterprise is built by wise planning, becomes strong through common sense, and profits wonderfully by keeping abreast of the facts.

He who grows older and wiser talks less and says more . . .

Proverbs 10:14

A wise man holds his tongue. Only a fool blurts out everything he knows; that only leads to sorrow and trouble.

He *who is a self-starter*
doesn't make a crank out
of his boss . . .

Proverbs 25:13

A faithful employee is as refreshing as a cool day
in the hot summertime.

He who hits
the ball over the fence
can take his time
going around the
bases . . .

Ecclesiastes 2:24,25

So I decided that there was nothing better for a
man to do than to enjoy his food and drink, and
his job. Then I realized that even this pleasure is
from the hand of God. For who can eat or enjoy
apart from him?

__He__ who never lets studying interfere with his education will have underwater grades—below C-level . . .

Proverbs 8:10-12

My instruction is far more valuable than silver or gold. For the value of wisdom is far above rubies; nothing can be compared with it. Wisdom and good judgment live together, for wisdom knows where to discover knowledge and understanding.

He who gives you free advice is probably charging you too much for it . . .

Proverbs 14:7

If you are looking for advice, stay away from fools.

He who is always shooting off his mouth is usually loaded with blanks . . .

Proverbs 15:28

A good man thinks before he speaks; the evil man pours out his evil words without a thought.

He who thinks he is a big shot is only a little shot who keeps on shooting . . .

Proverbs 26:12

Do you see a man wise in his own eyes? There is more hope for a fool than for him (NASB).

He who shows off usually gets showed up in a showdown . . .

1 Samuel 2:3,4

Quit acting so proud and arrogant! The Lord knows what you have done, and he will judge your deeds. Those who were mighty are mighty no more!

He who belongs to God is safe in His universe...

Proverbs 30:5

Every word of God proves true. He defends all who come to him for protection.

He who makes a start has half finished the job . . .

Proverbs 14:23

Work brings profit; talk brings poverty.

He who sows wild oats should not expect a crop failure...

Proverbs 11:29

The fool who provokes his family to anger and resentment will finally have nothing worthwhile left. He shall be the servant of a wiser man.

He who goes out of his way to get in yours is a pest . . .

Nehemiah 6:3

. . . I am doing a great work! Why should I stop to come and visit with you?

He who pays the piper calls the tunes . . .

Proverbs 19:4

A wealthy man has many "friends"; the poor man has none left.

He who knocks boldly brings good news.

Proverbs 13:17

An unreliable messenger can cause a lot of trouble. Reliable communication permits progress.

He *who laughs last may end up with a tooth missing...*

Ha Ha Ha we won!

Ecclesiastes 3:1,4

There is ... a time to cry; a time to laugh; a time to grieve; a time to dance ...

He who has butter-fingers should not try to climb the rope.

Proverbs 22:3

A prudent man foresees the difficulties ahead and prepares for them; the simpleton goes blindly on and suffers the consequences.

He who can't ride a gentle horse should not try to break a wild colt.

Proverbs 4:7

Determination to be wise is the first step toward becoming wise!

He who talks less and listens more will have less explaining to do.

Ecclesiastes 5:1,2

As you enter the Temple, keep your ears open and your mouth shut! Don't be a fool who doesn't even realize it is sinful to make rash promises to God, for he is in heaven and you are only here on earth, so let your words be few.

He who is a lazy butcher is a meat loafer . . .

Proverbs 13:4

Lazy people want much but get little, while the diligent are prospering.

He who gives while he lives also knows where it goes...

Proverbs 22:9

Happy is the generous man, the one who feeds the poor.

He who has the wheel determines the direction . . .

Proverbs 118:8

It is better to trust the Lord than to put confidence in men.

He who has a good aim in life must know how to pull the trigger...

Proverbs 4:25-27

Look straight ahead; don't even turn your head to look. Watch your step. Stick to the path and be safe. Don't sidetrack; pull back your foot from danger.

He *who teaches his children to swim when the basement is flooded is an opportunist.*

Ecclesiastes 3:1
There is a right time for everything . . .

He who gets someone else to blow his horn will find that the sound travels twice as far . . .

Proverbs 27:2

Don't praise yourself; let others do it!

He who pitches too high won't get through his song...

Proverbs 21:23

He who guards his mouth and his tongue, guards his soul from troubles (NASB).

He whose night-out is followed by a day-in is growing older . . .

Ecclesiastes 12:1

Don't let the excitement of being young cause you to forget about your Creator. Honor him in your youth before the evil years come . . .

He who is up to his waist in alligators is not looking for a way to drain the swamp . . .

Psalm 55:3,6,7

My enemies shout against me and threaten me with death. Oh, for wings like a dove, to fly away and rest! I would fly to the far off deserts and stay there.

He who doesn't know where he is going may miss it when he gets there . . .

You Are Lost

Proverbs 4:18,19

The good man walks along in the ever-brightening light of God's favor; the dawn gives way to morning splendor, while the evil man gropes and stumbles in the dark.

He who wants to finish the race must keep on tracking...

Ecclesiastes 7:8

Finishing is better than starting! Patience is better than pride!

He who is alone is not necessarily in good company...

Ecclesiastes 4:9,10

Two can accomplish more than twice as much as one, for the results can be much better. If one falls, the other pulls him up; but if a man falls when he is alone, he's in trouble.

He who will cheat you at play will cheat you in other ways...

Proverbs 11:1

The Lord hates cheating and delights in honesty.

He who is footloose and fiancée-free is a bachelor...

Proverbs 4:23

Above all else, guard your affections. For they influence everything else in your life.

He who brings home the bacon without spilling the beans is a true diplomat...

Proverbs 25:15

Be patient and you will finally win, for a soft tongue can break hard bones.

He who puts his head in
a sauna and his feet in a
deep freeze will feel pretty
good—on the average . . .

Ecclesiastes 7:14

Enjoy prosperity whenever you can, and when
hard times strike, realize that God gives one as
well as the other . . .

He who has a good conscience has a continual Christmas . . .

Proverbs 15:15

When a man is gloomy, everything seems to go wrong; when he is cheerful, everything seems right!

He who falls in love with himself will have no competition . . .

Proverbs 26:12

There is one thing worse than a fool, and that is a man who is conceited.

He who lives without songs is like a wagon without springs...

Proverbs 29:6
Good men . . . sing for joy.

He who wants to save face should keep the lower part shut . . .

Proverbs 17:27,28

The man of few words and settled mind is wise; therefore, even a fool is thought to be wise when he is silent. It pays him to keep his mouth shut.

He who gets on a high horse is riding for a fall...

I think I need a shorter horse.

Proverbs 28:13

A man who refuses to admit his mistakes can never be successful. But if he confesses and forsakes them, he gets another chance.

He who has clenched fists cannot shake hands...

Proverbs 22:24,25

Keep away from angry, short-tempered men, lest you learn to be like them and endanger your soul.

He who thinks he has no faults has at least one . . .

Ecclesiastes 7:20

And there is not a single man in all the earth who is always good and never sins.

He who goes on a diet must first remember to forget seconds . . .

Proverbs 23:1,2

When dining with a rich man, be on your guard and don't stuff yourself, though it all tastes so good . . .

He **who doesn't read good books has no advantage over the person who cannot read them . . .**

Psalm 119:18-20

Open my eyes to see wonderful things in your Word. I am but a pilgrim here on earth: how I need a map—and your commands are my chart and guide. I long for your instructions more than I can tell.

He who does a good day's work seldom has to worry about a good night's sleep...

Ecclesiastes 5:12

The man who works hard sleeps well whether he eats little or much, but the rich must worry and suffer insomnia.

He who thinks it's okay to tell white lies will soon go colorblind...

Psalm 101:7

But I will not allow those who deceive and lie to stay in my house.

He who deals with the devil will make small profits...

Proverbs 11:18

The evil man gets rich for the moment, but the good man's reward lasts forever.

He who claims to be a self-made man is in love with his creator...

Ecclesiastes 8:17

...Of course, only God can see everything, and even the wisest man who says he knows everything, doesn't.

He *who hunts two rabbits will catch neither...*

Psalm 32:8

I will instruct you (says the Lord) and guide you
along the best pathway for your life; I will advise
you and watch your progress.

He who remembers a
woman's birthday but not
her age is a tactful
man . . .

Proverbs 3:4,5

If you want favor with both God and man, and a
reputation for good judgment and common sense,
then trust the Lord completely; don't ever trust
yourself.

He who says "What's the use?" is never the engine, always the caboose . . .

Proverbs 12:24

Work hard and become a leader; be lazy and never succeed.

He who overindulges
soon bulges...

Proverbs 23:19,20

O my son, be wise and stay in God's paths; don't
carouse with drunkards and gluttons, for they are
on their way to poverty.

Ecclesiastes 9:12

A man never knows when he is going to run into bad luck. He is like a fish caught in a net, or a bird caught in a snare.

He who doesn't touch the rope will not ring the bell...

Proverbs 12:1

To learn, you must want to be taught. To refuse reproof is stupid.

He who takes a journey of 1000 miles begins with one step...

Exodus 14:15

Then the Lord said to Moses, "Quit praying and get the people moving! Forward, march!"

He who does not rise early never does a good day's work...

Psalm 5:3

Each morning I will look to you in heaven and lay my requests before you, praying earnestly.

He who swells in prosperity will shrink in adversity...

Proverbs 24:10

You are a poor specimen if you can't stand the pressure of adversity.

He who has to eat his own words never asks for a second helping . . .

Proverbs 21:23; 29:11

Keep your mouth closed and you'll stay out of trouble. A rebel shouts in anger; a wise man holds his temper in and cools it.

He who kills time should learn to work it to death instead...

Psalm 90:12

Teach us to number our days and recognize how few they are; help us to spend them as we should.

***He* who blows on the coals in quarrels he has nothing to do with has no right to complain if the sparks fly in his face . . .**

Proverbs 15:1

A soft answer turns away wrath, but harsh words cause quarrels.

He who expects something for nothing will have to wait until Easter falls on Tuesday...

Proverbs 12:9

It is better to get your hands dirty—and eat, than to be too proud to work—and starve.

He who wants to be a live wire on the job must find a place to recharge . . .

Isaiah 40:31

They that wait upon the Lord shall renew their strength. They shall mount up with wings like eagles; they shall run and not be weary; they shall walk and not faint.

He *who covers his chair instead of his territory finds himself at the bottom most of the time . . .*

Proverbs 10:26

A lazy fellow is a pain to his employers—like smoke in their eyes or vinegar that sets the teeth on edge.

He who is all wrapped up in himself is overdressed . . .

Proverbs 11:2

Proud men end in shame, but the meek become wise.

He who speaks when he is angry makes the best speech he'll ever regret . . .

Proverbs 11:9

Evil words destroy. Godly skill rebuilds.

He who goes places and boos things is a critic...

Too tart... not enough sweetness, much too much pulp, too much ice, all in all I'd give it a C minus.

LEMONADE
5¢

Proverbs 8:13

Wisdom hates pride, arrogance, corruption and deceit of every kind.

He who eats forbidden fruit will end up in a jam...

Proverbs 12:21

No real harm befalls the good, but there is constant trouble for the wicked.

He who prays for rain should not leave home without his umbrella...

Psalm 84:5,6

Happy are those who are strong in the Lord, who want above all else to follow your steps. When they walk through the Valley of Weeping it will become a place of springs where pools of blessing and refreshment collect after the rains!

He who jumps to conclusions usually has a rough landing...

Proverbs 18:13,17

What a shame—yes, how stupid!—to decide before knowing the facts! Any story sounds true until someone tells the other side and sets the record straight.

He who reaches the end of his rope should tie a knot and hold on . . .

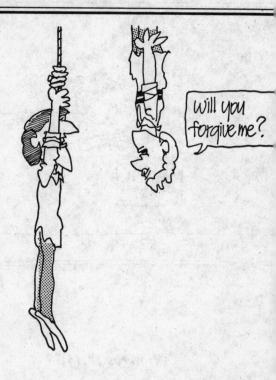

Proverbs 16:32

It is better to be slow-tempered than famous; it is better to have self-control than to control an army.

He who stretches the truth soon discovers that it snaps back...

Psalm 34:12,13

Do you want a long, good life? Then watch your tongue! Keep your lips from lying.

Other Good
Harvest House Reading

QUIPS, QUOTES, AND QUESTS
by *Vern McLellan*

You will never be without a wise or witty saying after you read *Quips, Quotes, and Quests*. This compilation of famous (and infamous) Bible verses, quotations, and sayings is a handy reference for the whole family.

PROVERBS, PROMISES, AND PRINCIPLES
by *Vern McLellan*

A stimulating new collection of thought-provoking sayings and colorful anecdotes to give your life and conversation a lift. Contains hundreds of new topics handled in a skillful and readable style. By the author of *Quips, Quotes, and Quests*.

PROVERBS FOR PEOPLE
by *Vern McLellan*

Clever proverbs are matched with a corresponding Scripture reference and illustration that will bring a smile and a cause for reflection with the turn of each page.

SHREDDED WIT
by *Vern McLellan*

Crisp, crackling, popping-good one liners from the author of *Proverbs for People* and *Quips, Quotes, and Quests*. A "bran" new serving of insightful bitefuls of wit and wisdom. Supplement your diet with hundreds of delightful and inspirational morsels of high fiber humor. Over 100,000 Vern McLellan books now in print!

THE BEST OF THE GOOD CLEAN JOKES
by *Bob Phillips*

Bestselling humorist Bob Phillips compiles the "best of the best" in his newest collection of wholesome humor. Preachers, teachers, family, and friends—anyone who enjoys good clean jokes—won't want to miss this laugh-filled resource from the pen of the master joker.

THE WORLD'S GREATEST COLLECTION OF DAFFY DEFINITIONS/RIDDLES
by *Bob Phillips*

In this double-dose of laughs, you'll find riddles on topics ranging from time, food, and love to spelling and children *OR* turn the book over and enjoy the latest and greatest collection of crazy "one-liners" yet assembled by the master compiler of wit and humor.

GETTING IN TOUCH WITH GOD
by *Jim Burns*

Written with the insightful style that has made Jim Burns so popular among young people, this daily devotional hits on timely topics confronting every believer. Jim takes you to Scripture and practical application in such areas as love, prayer, the Holy Spirit, and the promises of God. Dynamic in its approach yet highly relevant, this devotional has tremendous potential to bring live to your quiet times alone with God.

DATING YOUR MATE
by *Rick Bundschuh* and *Dave Gilbert*

If you've ever longed to return to those wonderful, fun-filled days of "courting," then *Dating Your Mate* is for you and your spouse. Chock-full of clever ideas that will put the romance, excitement, and spontaneity back in your life, *Dating Your Mate* is a practical guide to creative fun for marrieds and yet-to-be-marrieds. Delightfully illustrated by the authors.

Dear Reader:

We would appreciate hearing from you regarding this Harvest House nonfiction book. It will enable us to continue to give you the best in Christian publishing.

1. What most influenced you to purchase *Wise Words from a Wise Guy*?
   ☐ Author   ☐ Recommendations
   ☐ Subject matter   ☐ Cover/Title
   ☐ Backcover copy   ☐ _____

2. Where did you purchase this book?
   ☐ Christian bookstore   ☐ Grocery store
   ☐ General bookstore   ☐ Other
   ☐ Department store

3. Your overall rating of this book:
   ☐ Excellent   ☐ Very good   ☐ Good   ☐ Fair   ☐ Poor

4. How likely would you be to purchase other books by this author?
   ☐ Very likely   ☐ Not very likely
   ☐ Somewhat likely   ☐ Not at all

5. What types of books most interest you?
   (check all that apply)
   ☐ Women's Books   ☐ Fiction
   ☐ Marriage Books   ☐ Biographies
   ☐ Current Issues   ☐ Children's Books
   ☐ Self Help/Psychology   ☐ Youth Books
   ☐ Bible Studies   ☐ Other _____

6. Please check the box next to your age group.
   ☐ Under 18   ☐ 25-34   ☐ 45-54
   ☐ 18-24   ☐ 35-44   ☐ 55 and over

Mail to: Editorial Director
Harvest House Publishers, Inc.
1075 Arrowsmith
Eugene, OR 97402

Name _____

Address _____

City _____ State _____ Zip _____

Thank you for helping us to help you in future publications!